KEYS TO L
RESEARCH ON THE
GRADUATE LEVEL

A Guide to Guides

Harvey R. Gover

UNIVERSITY
PRESS OF
AMERICA

DEDICATION

To

All those whose enthusiasm, support,
and hard work helped make this guidebook possible.

iv

ACKNOWLEDGEMENTS

A special expression of gratitude is due to Linda Land, Joy Riherd, and Sue Barckhoff for their painstaking care in preparation of the manuscript; to Helen Hudson for her encouragement and invaluable aid over the phone; to those Tarleton graduate students who read and critiqued the manuscript, especially Joyce Ford, Ann Richey, and Linda Wade; to those Tarleton professors for whose classes this guidebook was first prepared: Dr. Ronald D. Bradberry, Dr. William C. Swindle, Dr. Johnny M. Johnson, Dr. Alice J. Cushman, Dr. Charles Jeremy Curtoys, and Dr. George Housewright; and to our Library Director, Mr. Henry T. Lohrmann, for his encouragement of the library orientation program.

Contents

PREFACE

Suddenly you are a graduate student, and all at once, more is expected of you - a consistently higher level of academic performance; and more is assumed of you - that you have attained skills of study and self expression far superior to those which you brought to college as a freshman. These requirements for expertise have become more complex today than ever before as the frontiers of human knowledge have been pushed back; as the actual amount of information has increased geometrically; and as the level and kind of technical skills required of professional people in all fields, even the most tradition bound, have grown significantly.

All this means that you will very soon find yourself required to do a lot of high-level library research for which you may feel unprepared. This guide is designed to get you started - and give you a solid start. You might call it the graduate student's library survival kit.

First of all, don't feel bad if you are bewildered at this point. Even experienced students and specialists have found themselves overwhelmed by exposure to the ever increasing amount and growing complexity of material now available. These scholars and professionals know that they are responsible for sifting through all this material and drawing upon it with accurate, appropriate selectivity, if they are to achieve the meaningful study necessary to continuing intellectual growth.

Second, get your money's worth; this kit will prove of little value to you, unless you follow through on its suggestions. Just reading the kit is not enough. You must go to the libraries on your campus to examine and use the tools and services covered here before the kit can prove genuinely beneficial.

x

THE CAMPUS LIBRARY SYSTEM

Full access to appropriate research materials on a university campus requires an overall knowledge of its library facilities. Most university campuses are covered with a network of departmental libraries that operate in conjunction with one or two much larger main libraries. If there is more than one main library, then one of them is often designated for use primarily by undergraduates and the other for use by graduate students, professors, and specialists.

This scattering of materials and services can cause serious complications for graduate students who often must draw upon materials from all levels. On such a campus the student faces the dual problem of learning both what the appropriate materials are and where these materials are housed.

Fortunately, where branch libraries exist, each graduate level program tends to have its own branch or departmental library which will contain most and in some cases all the materials the student will require. Wherever this is the case, the student's research problems are greatly simplified. However, branch libraries by their very nature are limited in scope and content, and research problems requiring a wide range of sources will take the student outside a departmental branch. It is necessary, then, for the student to become familiar with the content and arrangement of the university libraries throughout the campus.

For instance, the graduate student will need to learn whether or not there is a central catalog listing all books owned by the university and indicating in what library each is held. There should also be some sort of directory or guidebook available that lists the campus libraries, gives their location, and a brief description of their contents. Each of these libraries should in turn provide some kind of

1

individual guidance, perhaps in printed form, and certainly from its staff.

THE LIBRARY INFORMATION STAFF

Before discussing library information tools, it is appropriate to mention those library staff members who are primarily responsible for helping students locate information. Every academic library provides at least one professional specialist on duty during service hours, and larger libraries employ whole teams of them. A desk in a prominant spot in the library's public service area is usually marked "Reference" or "Information." At this desk students may seek aid in locating appropriate materials. In fact, no matter how simple or how complex the question may be, students should not hesitate to seek help from the library information staff, since helping students is their primary responsibility. In addition to helping with specific problems, information departments are increasingly providing general guidance through locally prepared brochures, tapes, programs, etc. These describe exactly how materials have been arranged in their own library. In fact, there is a national movement underway in all types of libraries, especially academic ones, to provide optimum conditions for physical, intellectual, and bibliographical access to their holdings. A central thrust and focus of this movement has been to prepare an informed library user through user education programs. These programs include printed, self-guided tours; casette self guided tours, video tape presentations; library lectures, tours, orientations, and seminars. Library education programs have been expanded, offer more depth, and occur on a more regular basis. Check to see what is available from your university libraries.

Although library information specialits are trained to help students on all levels who possess varying amounts of preparation and understanding of their subject matter and of the search process, the more knowledge about a research problem the student brings with him, and the more knowledge of how to go about the search process, the better able he will be to articulate his needs to a library professional. This brochure is designed to give students a sense of independence in doing library work as well as to enhance their ability to seek aid effectively.

THE CARD CATALOG AND
BASIC PERIODICAL INDEXES

Skills in using the card catalog and basic periodical indexes are essential for locating information on any level of research. Without these skills even a smaller library can seem a vast wilderness of unmanageable and unattainable material. A number of guides to the use of the card catalog and basic periodical indexes are available. Campus book stores usually have a section set aside for general library and research guides. If there is a particular guide that you want which is not regularly kept in stock, the bookstore should be able to order it for you. There should also be copies of this type of general guide available for loan in your main campus library. If so, these will be listed under the subject heading "Libraries - Handbooks, Manuals, etc." An information librarian can assist you. In fact, looking for this kind of guidebook should make an excellent beginning exercise. In addition, as mentioned earlier, many academic libraries provide their own locally prepared guidance packages to their card catalog and to their own unique arrangement of sources. The information librarian can also let you know about these. Here are two nationally published library guidebooks which offer valuable, detailed aid:

Robert B. Downs and Clara D. Keller. How to Do
     Library Research. 2nd. ed. University of
     Illinois Press, 1975.

Mona McCormick. Who-What-When-Where-How-Why-Made
     Easy. Time Books, 1971. Also in paper-
     back under the title New York Times Guide
     to Reference Materials.

Both books are available in bound and paperback editions. Unfortunately, neither one is complete enough in itself to be used alone. When used together though, these two books offer clear initial directions for the beginning researcher.

Downs and Keller's chapter two on the card catalog and classification systems is superior; however, some items discussed by McCormick do not appear there. Downs and Keller's chapter five on periodicals is too inadequate and must be supplemented by the specific examples of pages and entries supplied by McCormick's chapter on newspapers and periodicals. McCormick's guidance in using basic indexes can be applied to the more specialized ones in the student's field.

Neither of these guides discussed the card catalog or periodical indexes in enough detail to meet a graduate student's needs. These guides do not cover all the necessary details even when taken together or in combination with the half a dozen or so others available on the market from book publishers. The value of these works lies in their providing the graduate student with the essential initial steps without which pursuit of more complex research problems would be impossible.

One final word about the two guidebooks listed above: Both offer lists of references designed to carry the student beyond the card catalog and basic periodical indexes. McCormick's book, however, discusses references that are on a general level of interest and of academic use largely only to undergraduates. Downs and Keller by contrast include a wide range of fields and list works of importance to graduate level study within each field. If Downs and Keller include an area of study, then the works covered under it will offer a first step toward learning its graduate reference material.

WHAT THE GUIDEBOOKS WON'T TELL YOU

Preparation of this survival kit included
examining every major nationally marketed library
guidebook available today. Although a few points
omitted in some guides were covered in others, a
number of items especially important for graduate
students were absent in all of them. The following sections are devoted to those essential items.

The Card Catalog

First, let's look at the card catalog as
a physical entity, because that's how you the student will approach it. The catalog, as you have
no doubt already experienced it, consists of cabinets divided into little drawers usually referred
to as trays. Inside the trays, cards are arranged
in alphabetical order by author, title, and subject. In some libraries the authors, titles, and
subjects are separated from each other into dis-
tinct sections with each section labeled according
to its contents. This is known as a divided catalog. If you are accustomed to this type of setup,
then you will look for the section label you want
before looking for the specific item. However, not
every library divides its catalog. Many small libraries and even a few larger ones combine authors,
titles, and subjects into one alphabetical sequence.
In this case there are no separate sections or
section labels. You are looking only for the tray
that holds the exact beginning combination of
letters for the word you need, whether it is an
author's last name, the first main word in the
title of a book or a subject word. Rarely will
you be in a library so small that all the cards
having entries beginning with one letter of the
alphabet can be put into just one tray, whether
the catalog is divided or not. The cards for words
beginning with one letter will continue through
several trays, so you will need to look for the
tray that holds the exact combination of beginning
letters, that is, the first three or four letters
for the word or name you need.

Either type of card catalog, divided or non-divided, presents its special problems to the user. Take people's names for instance. Libraries will own books both by and about well known individuals. With a divided catalog, the words by a person will be entered under that person's name in the author section, but there are variations in the placement of works about the person. In some cases, words about the individual are also grouped in the author section following the works by that person. In other cases, the cards for works-about are treated as subject cards and are filed in the subject section. Still another technique places works-about in a separate biographical section.

With a non-divided catalog, works by and about the author naturally fall together alphabetically under his or her name. This necessitates some device for differentiating works-by from works-about. Works-by are therefore usually placed ahead of works-about. There may even be a guide card separating the two, indicating where the works-about begin. Color coding is another effective means whereby the works-about have the person's name added in red at the top of the card. This lets the user know immediately that a card having the person's name added in red at the top is for a book about the person.

The color coding in a non-divided catalog will then be carried over to other types of subject cards, so that all subject words can easily be distinguished from words in titles on title cards. Let's look at some relevant examples.

Example 1 is the author card for Walter Brylowski's book Faulkner's Olympian Laugh, a book of criticism about the works of the famous American novelist William Faulkner. This particular card is called the author card, because it is filed under Brylowski's name, it being the uppermost entry on the card. If you wanted this book and knew that Brylowski had written it, you could look it up under his last name.

8

```
PS3511
A86Z65   Brylowski, Walter.
            Faulkner's Olympian laugh; myth in the
         novels.  Detroit, Wayne State University Press,
         1968.

            236 p.  24 cm.

            Bibliography:  p. 230-232.


            1.  Faulkner, William, 1897-1962.  1.  Title.
         PS3511.A86Z65              813'.5'2        68--11137

         Library of Congress
```

Example 1

However, people frequently do not know or
do not remember the author's name; hence, the in-
clusion in the catalog of title cards. Subject
cards are provided for times when no specific
authors or titles are known ahead of time. Since
the book in Example 1 is about an accomplished
author, and its title begins with the author's
last name, it presents a complicated, though not
unusual alphabetizing case, whether for a divided
or non-divided catalog.

Example 2 shows a typical arrangement for
the subject of Brylowski's book in an undivided
catalog. Since William Faulkner is the subject,
his name will be added, probably in red, at the
top of a card and that card will be placed along
with other cards having Faulkner's name at the
top, some of which will be works by him, others
about him. In this case works by him are inter-
filed alphabetically with works about him and
color coded to distinguish them effectively.

Card A in Example 2 shows a work by Faulkner, his novel, A Fable. Card B is the subject
card for our book Faulkner's Olympian Laugh. In

May be added
    in red

```
                                              Card D
          Faulkner, William, 1897-1962
              Light in August
  PS3511
  A86L575 Minter, David L          Comp.
          Twentieth century interpretations of Light
          in August;...
```

```
                                              Card C
  PZ3
  F272Li3 Faulkner, William, 1897-1962.
          Light in August.  Introd. by Richard H.
```

May be added
    in red

```
                                              Card B
          Faulkner, William, 1897-1962
  PS3511
  A86Z5   Brylowski, Walter.
          Faulkner's Olympian laugh; myth in the
          novels,
```

```
                                              Card A
  PZ3
  F272Fab Faulkner, William, 1897-1962
          A fable. [New York] Random House [1954]

          437 p.  22 cm.




          1.  European War, 1914-1918--Fiction.
          I.  Title.
          PZ3.F272Fab                          54-6651

          Library of Congress
```

Example 2

some libraries this card will be alphabetized
first under Faulkner, William, 1897-1962, and
then subarranged by "Brylowski, Walter." In
others, the "Brylowski, Walter" is disregarded
and "Faulkner's Olympian..." is used; so we see
in Example 3 with the Brylowski arbitrarily
omitted, the simplified order with "Fable" preceding "Faulkner's."

Faulkner, William, 1897-1962
    Faulkner's Olympian...

Faulkner, William, 1897-1962
    A fable.

Example 3

        Now we'll take a look at Cards C and D in
Example 2. Card C is the author card for Faulkner's fiction work Light in August. Card D immediately following Card C is the subject card for
a book of criticism of Light in August. This subject card not only lets the user know that Faulkner is the subject of the book, but also the card
goes on to indicate that the book is about one
particular work by Faulkner in adding both Faulkner's name and the title of his work discussed at
the top of the card. Under the filing system
shown here, this criticism of Light in August
follows immediately behind the card for the work
itself. In a divided catalog, of course this
might not be the case. Nevertheless, this type
of entry for the criticism of a specific work
should be used in all card catalogs, regardless of
where it is placed, and you should be able to re-
cognize it whenever you encounter it.

11

So far, we have talked about the author card and the subject card for Brylowski's Faulkner's Olympian Laugh. Example 4 shows the title card in an alphabetical context. If you knew the exact title of this book, you would not want to wade through all the "Faulkner, William" as subject entries for it. You would rather go directly to that title entry. To do so, you need to know that in a word by word alphabetical arrangement, "Faulkner's" with an "s" is placed after Faulkner, so you would bypass all the "Faulkner, William" entries and all entries for titles beginning with "Faulkner" to find those beginning with "Faulkners" or "Faulkner's," which in turn fall together in order according to the word which follows each. In Example 4 "Faulkners of..." precedes "Faulkner's Olympian...." These examples would hold true whether found in the titles of a divided catalog or alphabetized in an undivided one.

Before leaving Brylowski's book, let's take another look at the cards placed in the catalog for it. Example 5 has these three cards lined up for a closer look. Notice that the cards are identical except for the addition of the title on one and the person as subject on another. They are identical because these cards are preprinted as a set and sold to libraries by the Library of Congress which prints its name at the bottom of the card. Similar sets are also printed by commercial firms which prepare materials to aid libraries in their cataloging procedures. Buying preprinted sets is less costly than having them prepared and typed locally. Notice that also given at the bottom of the card are the Library of Congress and Dewey decimal numbers for this book. Both numbers are printed at the bottom of the card, since libraries using both systems are going to be purchasing the book and the catalog cards for the book. No number is printed in the upper left hand corner of the card, so that each library purchasing the book and cards can put whichever number it is using there. Also, the way in which

```
Ref         Faulkner's people                Card C
PS3511
A86Z87   Kirk, Robert Warner.
            Faulkner's people, a complete guide and index
```

```
            Faulkner's Olympian laugh           Card B
PS3511
A86Z65   Brylowski, Walter.
            Faulkner's Olympian laugh; myth in novels.
```

```
            The Faulkners of Mississippi        Card A
PS3511
A86Z7832  Falkner, Murry C., 1899-
            The Falkners of Mississippi, a memior by
          Murry C. Falkner.  Baton Rouge, Louisiana
          State University Press [1967]

            xxv,  205 p.  illus.,  ports.  23 cm.



            1.  Faulkner, William, 1897-1962.  I.  Title.

          PS3511.A86Z7832          813'.52 (B)   67--24417

          Library of Congress
```

Note the variation in spelling
to make the added title conform
to all the others for the same
author.

                    Example 4

                        13

the number is typed in this corner and on the label that is placed on the spine of the book varies from library to library. To illustrate, the
PS3511 is written as one line on these cards in
Example 5, but it is frequently written with the
PS above the 3511. Notice, too, that the decimal
preceding the A86 in Example 5 has been eliminated when the number was transposed to the upper
left corner. It usually is written as shown
below:

```
            PS              PS
            3511            3511
            .A86Z65         .A86
                            Z65
```

```
PS3511
A86Z65   Brylowski, Walter.
              Faulkner's Olympian laugh; myth in the novels.
         Detroit, Wayne State University Press, 1968.

              236 p.  24 cm.

              Bibliography:  p. 230-232.

                 1.  Faulkner, William, 1897-1962.  I.  Title
           PS3511.A86Z65              813'.5'2      68--11137

                  Library of Congress
```

Recommended subject entry	Dewey Decimal classification number	Recommends making title entry

Library of Congress   Library of Congress
classification number   processing number

Example 5, Part 1

14

```
┌─────────────────────────────────────────────────────────────┐
│          Faulkner's Olympian laugh                          │
│ PS3511                                                       │
│ A86Z65   Brylowski, Walter.                                 │
│             Faulkner's Olympian laugh; myth in the novels.  │
│          Detroit, Wayne State University Press, 1968.       │
│                                                              │
│             236 p.  24 cm.                                  │
│                                                              │
│             Bibliography:  p. 230-232.                      │
│                                                              │
│                                                              │
│             1.  Faulkner, William, 1897-1962.  I.  Title.  │
│          PS3511.A8Z65              813'.5'2      68-11137    │
│                            ◯                                 │
│          Library of Congress                                 │
└─────────────────────────────────────────────────────────────┘
```

```
┌─────────────────────────────────────────────────────────────┐
│          Faulkner, William,  1897-1962.                     │
│ PS3511                                                       │
│ A86Z65   Brylowski, Walter.                                 │
│             Faulkner's Olympian laugh; myth in the novels.  │
│          Detroit, Wayne State University Press, 1968.       │
│                                                              │
│             236 p.  24 cm.                                  │
│                                                              │
│             Bibliography:  p. 230-232.                      │
│                                                              │
│                                                              │
│             1.  Faulkner, William, 1897-1962.  I.  Title.  │
│          PS3511.A86Z65             813'.5'2    68--11137     │
│                            ◯                                 │
│          Library of Congress                                 │
└─────────────────────────────────────────────────────────────┘
```

Example 5, Part 2

15

Also shown on the bottom of each card are the recommended subject headings, in this case the name of the person who is the subject of the book, and a recommendation that a title card be made. These recommendations are known as tracings and are placed there for use by librarians, but can be most helpful to students. Let's take a look at an example having regular subject words rather than a person as subject.

Examples 6 and 7 show the set of cards for Moelwyn-Hughes's States of Matter. Notice the amount of information that is repeated on each card. In the tracings three subject headings are recommended. These headings appear at the top of each card in Example 7. Now let's see how the tracings can be used to the student's advantage. Let's say that you have been assigned a paper on molecular dynamics and your professor tells you that at least six or eight book references must be used. He further suggests that Moelwyn-Hughes is an authority in this field, and if you can locate some of his works, they will be most helpful to you. Therefore, you look in the card catalog under the author's name, and you find Card A in Example 6.

Using the call number given on Card A, you go to the QC173 section of the library and there you locate States of Matter and four other books on molecular dynamics. This gives you five books, but you were told to use at least six or eight, so you can go back to the author card of the book, look down at the tracings and learn exactly what headings to look for in order to locate additional material. You learn in this case that in addition to molecular dynamics, you can also look under Matter-Constitution or Chemical equilibrium.

Knowing this eliminated your having to speculate and search through various possible subject words or phrases, some of which may not actually appear in the card catalog. If you have ever spent hours searching through subject head-

16

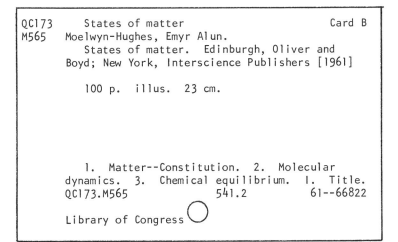

```
QC173                                          Card A
M565    Moelwyn-Hughes, Emyr Alun.
           States of matter.  Edinburgh, Oliver and
        Boyd; New York, Interscience Publishers [1961]

           100 p.  illus.  23 cm.




           1.  Matter--Constitution.  2.  Molecular
        dynamics.  3.  Chemical equilibrium.  I.  Title.
        QC173.M565              541.2          61-66822

        Library of Congress
```

```
QC173     States of matter                    Card B
M565    Moelwyn-Hughes, Emyr Alun.
           States of matter.  Edinburgh, Oliver and
        Boyd; New York, Interscience Publishers [1961]

           100 p.  illus.  23 cm.




           1.  Matter--Constitution.  2.  Molecular
        dynamics.  3.  Chemical equilibrium.  I.  Title.
        QC173.M565              541.2          61--66822

        Library of Congress
```

Example 6

17

```
QC173      Matter - Constitution                  Card B
M565       Moelwyn-Hughes, Emry Alun.
               States of matter.  Edinburgh, Oliver and Boyd;
           New York, Interscience Publishers [1961]

               100 p.  illus.  23 cm.




               1.  Matter--Constitution.  2.  Molecular
           dynamics.  3.  Chemical equilibrium.  I.  Title.
           QC173.M565                541.2              61-66822

           Library of Congress
```

```
QC173      Molecular dynamics                     Card A
M565       Moelwyn-Hughes, Emyr Alun.
               States of matter.  Edinburgh, Oliver and Boyd;
           New York, Interscience Publishers [1961]

               100 p.  illus.  23 cm.




               1.  Matter--Constitution.  2.  Molecular
           dynamics.  3.  Chemical equilibrium.  I.  Title.
           QC173.M565                541.2              61--66822

           Library of Congress
```

Example 7, Part 1

18

```
QC173      Chemical equilibrium                    Card C
M565       Moelwyn-Hughes, Emyr Alun.
                States of matter.  Edinburgh, Oliver and Boyd;
           New York, Interscience Publishers [1961]

                100 p.  illus.  23 cm.




                1.  Matter--Constitution.  2.  Molecular
           dynamics.  3.  Chemical equilibrium.  I.  Title.
           QC173.M565              541.2              61--66822

           Library of Congress  (   )
```

Example 7, Part 2

ings looking for appropriate ones, then you can
see right away how helpful and time saving knowing
about the tracings and how to use them can be.
Looking under Chemical equilibrium, for instance,
revealed several slightly different call numbers
from the original QC173, that would not be readily
evident working just from this original number.
Other numbers included QD501, QD81, and QD541.

    Notice that since the tracings appear at
the bottom of every card, it does not matter
where you begin with your first book. You could
just as easily have been told by your professor
that a book entitled States of Matter would be most
helpful to you, and you could have initiated the
process of searching for additional references by
looking at the tracings at the bottom of the title
card after having located it.

    The same would be true if you had not
known about any one particular book on molecular
dynamics. You could simply have looked under molecular dynamics, located the books listed under

that heading and then looked at the tracings on
any one of them, like Card A in Example 7, to take
you on to still other books with varying numbers.

An additional problem in searching for
materials by subject is that the word a student
has chosen for that subject is often not the same
word used for listing the books on it in the card
catalog. The catalogers try to anticipate this
problem in advance and place cards in the catalog
known as "see references," giving the student's
word or phrase and telling which alternate word or
phrase was actually used for the subject, thereby
telling the student where to look to find the materials needed.

Besides the "see" reference card, one
other type of referral card is provided known as
a "see also" card. The "see also" card follows a
subject card and tells the student of at least one
other word or phrase to look under for additional
related books. Downs and Keller give examples of
"see" and "see also" references, but do not explain their value and usefulness to the student.
"See also" references can be helpful when the student has not been able to locate enough material
and needs to go to look under additional subject
listings. "See also" references, therefore, serve
the same purpose for the student as the tracings
at the bottom of cards when these are consulted
for additional subject references.

What we have said so far in discussing the
card catalog as a physical entity applies to the
traditional library card catalog with its wood
cabinets and trays full of individual cards. Large
academic libraries will no doubt continue to main-
tain and expand these catalogs at least for the
near future, but eventually such catalogs will
become a part of the past.

Newer college libraries founded in recent
years have not established card catalogs but have
stored the information for their book holdings on

20

microfiche to be read by library users with microfiche readers. Library patrons are given instruc-
tions on how to use the microfiche and readers.
Such catalogs are often kept up to date with
printed supplements until the additional microfiche can be prepared and added. The user will
need to inquire about how the catalog is kept up
to date.

In some cases the information provided is
very similar to that given on the traditional
catalog cards. Tracings appear, for instance, and
can be used for additional subject headings. With
other microfiche catalogs the entries are more
abbreviated and one cannot take advantage of such
features as tracings, because these details have
been eliminated. In fact, the information provided by the microfiche catalog can be so re-
structured from the traditional catalog cards that
some orientation may be necessary for new users.

In the very near future pilot programs
will be set up in a few larger academic libraries
which will feature terminals for on-line access
to library catalogs stored by computer. Library
users will be taught to key-in requests for the
desired information from the catalog data base.
This information will appear on cathode-ray tubes
with the possible option of making paper copies
of the screen images. Again, user orientation will
be necessary. The value to library users of on-
line access lies in the greater flexibility for
searching that these systems afford, especially
for graduate level students who will need to know
all the options available to them in terms of the
books and various editions of the books from which
they may choose. Watch for such developments on
your campus.

Similar advancements will no doubt be
appearing on your campus, soon, perhaps during your
career as a graduate student. Nevertheless, years
will be required before these are widely available
and fully developed in large academic libraries.

21

In the meantime skills in using the card catalog are an absolute must. Perhaps the card catalog will always be necessary in older libraries, in large university libraries, and in special collections where the costs of conversion to machine stored data will be prohibitive.

Regardless of its format, the card catalog provides user access to books by giving the classification number of each book. Since the books are arranged on the library shelves according to these classification numbers, finding the books requires a knowledge of the structure of the classification system. The following section discusses structure and use of the Library of Congress classification.

THE LIBRARY OF CONGRESS CLASSIFICATION

Unfortunately, neither Downs and Keller nor McCormick provide an adequate discussion of the Library of Congress classification system. This is a serious omission, since the Library of Congress classification is used in most academic libraries in the United States today, having been introduced in the last decade. Knowledge of both the Dewey decimal classification and the Library of Congress is necessary, because not all libraries on any one university campus may have been converted from Dewey to L.C., and large collections that are being converted may not have completed the process, so will have some books still under Dewey and others under L.C. Fortunately, most people are familiar with the Dewey system from their elementary and secondary school, and public library experiences, but the Library of Congress classification is generally not encountered until the college or university level.

An excellent discussion of the Library of Congress classification may be found in:

Jean Key Gates. <u>Guide to the Use of Books and Libraries</u>. 3rd. ed. McGraw-Hill Book Co., 1974.

Ms. Gates points out that the Library of Congress classification was developed in 1897, somewhat later than Dewey's, which was first published in 1876, the American Centennial year. The Library of Congress adopted the new system to serve its own needs, but in setting up this new classification, the Library of Congress developed a system far more flexible than Dewey's. The L.C. system can simply accomodate the knowledge explosion more effectively than Dewey's, because it is infinitely more expandable, combining as it does letters of the alphabet with arabic numerals. The Dewey system, of course, uses numbers only in sets of tens and hundreds while the L.C. begins with twenty-one letters of the alphabet assigning

each letter to a major field or division of knowledge, then in turn subdivides each one of these
alphabetically. Each of the divisions and subdivisions is in turn broken down numerically in
whole number sequence from 1 through 9999. This
allows not only for expansion but also for minute,
detailed division of subjects, so that books on
very specific topics can each have their own subject number. The letters I, O, W, X, and Y are
being held in reserve for as yet undeveloped areas
of knowledge.

Gates provides an excellent basic outline
of the Library of Congress classification. Since
hers is the only major library guide providing
such a good outline, a similar one is provided
here in Example 8, in case students do not have
ready access to her work.

Notice that not all fields get a single
letter of their own. Psychology, for example,
was treated as an outgrowth of religion and philosophy, and was placed in the letter sequence under the B's, getting the pair of letters BF. Nor
was each individual field of the social sciences
assigned a letter of its own. Some were grouped
under H and assigned sequences of pairs of letters
such as economics having HB through HJ; and socio-
logy with related areas HM through HX.

Notice the divisions within the D classification on the first page of Example 8. These
basic divisions, as you can see, are geographical
by nation. Other fields use different types of
basic divisions according to what was appropriate
for each one. These basic divisions are designated by adding a second letter in alphabetical
order to the beginning or base letter. Notice
also that works too general to be put under one of
the basic divisions are simply assigned the single
letter. In this case general world histories are
just given the single letter D.

A further breakdown of the D classifica-

24

LIBRARY OF CONGRESS CLASSIFICATION

A. GENERAL WORKS-POLYGRAPHY
    Including encyclopedias, indexes, year-
    books, etc.

B. PHILOSOPHY-RELIGION
    B   Philosophy
    BF   Psychology
    BJ   Ethics
    BL-BX Religion, Theology

C. HISTORY-AUXILIARY SCIENCES
    CB-CN History of civilization,
           antiquities, archives,
           chronology, numismatics and
           coins, epigraphy

    CR-CT Heraldry, genealogy, biography
           (Not illustrative of any subject)

D. HISTORY AND TOPOGRAPHY (Except America)
    D   General History
    DA   Great Britain
    DB   Austria-Hungary
    DC   France
    DD   Germany
    DE   Classical Antiquity
    DF   Greece
    DG   Italy
    DH-DJ Netherlands
    DK   Russia
    DL   Scandinavia
    DP   Spain and Portugal
    DQ   Switzerland
    DR   Turkey and the Balkan States
    DS   Asia
    DT   Africa
    DU   Australia and Oceania
    DX   Gypsies

Example 8, Part 1

E.-F. AMERICA
       E   America (General) and United
                  States (General)
       F   United States (Local) and America
                  except United States, Canada
                  Mexico, Central and South America

G.   GEOGRAPHY-ANTHROPOLOGY
       G-GF   Geography, cartogrphy, ocean-
                  ography
       GN   Anthropology, Ethnology
       GR   Folk-lore
       GT   Manners and customs (General)
       GV   Sports and amusements, games

H.   SOCIAL SCIENCES
       H-HA   Social sciences (General) and
                  statistics
       HB-HJ   Economics including transportation
                  and communications, commerce
                  (General), finance and public
                  finance
       HM   Sociology (General), social
                  history, social groups, (Family,
                  Home, Communities), social
                  pathology and socialism, commu-
                  nism

J.   POLITICAL SCIENCE
       J-JC   Political science (General) theory
                  of state
       JK-JX   Constitutional history and admin-
                  istration, emigration, and immi-
                  gration, international law

K.   LAW

L.   EDUCATION
       L.   General works, history of educa-
                  tion, theory and practice, teach-
                  ing, special forms and applica-
                  tions, universities and colleges

Example 8, Part 2

26

M. MUSIC
  ML   Literature of music
  MT   Instruction and study

N. FINE ARTS
  NA   Architecture
  NB   Sculpture
  NC   Grphic arts in general
  ND   Painting
  NE   Engraving
  NK   Arts applied to industry;
       decoration and ornament

P. LANGUAGE AND LITERATURE
  P   Philology and linguistics (General)
  PA   Classical Languages and Literature
  PB   Modern European Languages
  PC   Romance Languages
  PD   Germanic (Teutonic) Languages
  PE   English, Anglo-Saxon, Middle
       English
  PF   Dutch, Flemish, Afrikaans
  PG   Slavic., Lithuanian-Lettish,
       Albanian Finno-Ugrian and Basque
       languages and literatures
  PJ-PK Oriental Languages and Literatures
  PL   Languages and Literatures of
       Eastern Asia, Oceania, Africa
  PM   Hyperborean, American, and
       Artificial Languages
  PN   Literary history and collections
       (General)
  PQ   Romance literature
  PR   English literature
  PS   American literature
  PT   Teutonic literature
  PZ   Fiction and Juvenile literature

Q. SCIENCES
  Q   Science (General)
  QA   Mathematics
  QB   Astronomy

Example 8, Part 3

27

```
QC          Physics
QD          Chemistry
QE          Geology
QH          Natural history
QK          Botany
QL          Zoology
QM          Human anatomy
QP          Physiology
QR          Bacteriology
```

R. MEDICINE
```
    R           Medicine (General)
                Including state medicine, hygiene,
                practice of medicine, therapeu-
                tics, pharmacy, nursing
```

S. AGRICULTURE - Plant and animal industry
```
    S           Agriculture (General)
    SB          Plant culture (General)
    SD          Forestry
    SF          Animal culture
    SH          Fish culture
    SK          Hunting sports
```

T. TECHNOLOGY
```
    TA-TH       Engineering and building group
    TJ-TL       Mechanical group
    TN-TR       Chemical group
    TS-TX       Composite group, manufactures,
                trade, domestic science
```

U. MILITARY SCIENCE

V. NAVAL SCIENCE

Z. BIBLIOGRAPHY AND LIBRARY SCIENCE

        Including history of books, writing, book
        industries and trade, copyright, libraries
        and library science, book prices, bibli-
        ography - National, subject and personal

                   Example 8, Part 4

                        28
```
```

tion is shown in Example 9. Note that when each
one of the basic divisions is subdivided, the
system begins to add numbers to letters. The
basic division, Great Britain, for example, gets
the letters DA. Each of its subdivisions is
assigned a sequence of numbers to be added to the
DA. Scotland, thereby, gets the series 750-890.

Let's take a closer look at the subdivision for Scotland. Our outline of the D classification is followed by an excerpt from the table
for Scotland, in Example 10, showing how individual numbers within a sequence are assigned to specific subdivisions. Notice that even further subdivisions can be made by adding decimal numbers to
a specific subdivision number. Decimal numbers
can in turn be further broken down by adding another decimal followed by a letter and number as
with House of Stuart (758.3.S8) under Houses, noble families, etc. (758.3).

Later we will discuss the importance of
knowing the literature of your field. The graduate student can gain an important introduction
to that literature by a careful examination of
the basic Library of Congress classification outline for his or her field. This outline provides
an overall structural or skeletal concept of the
field and may point out some avenues of research
and specialization that a student might not otherwise have realized existed within the philosophical framework of his field.

D

HISTORY and TOPOGRAPHY (except America)

```
D           General history
DA          Great Britain
                    20-690    England
                   700-745    Wales
                   750-890    Scotland
                   900-995    Ireland
DB          Austria-Hungary
DC          France
DD          Germany
DE          Classical antiquity
DF          Greece
DG          Italy
DH-DJ       Netherlands
            DH      1-207    Belgium and Holland
            DH    401-811    Belgium
            DH    901-925    Luxemburg (Grand duchy)
            DJ             Holland
DK          Russia
                     1-272    Russia (General)
                   401-441    Poland
                   445-465    Finland
                   750-891    Russia in Asia
DL          Scandinavia
                    1- 85    Scandinavia (General)
                   101-291    Denmark
                   301-398    Iceland
                   401-596    Norway
                   601-991    Sweden
DP          Spain and Portugal
                   1-402    Spain
                   501-900    Portugal
DQ          Switzerland
DR          Turkey and the Balkan States
DS          Asia
DT          Africa
DU          Australia and Oceania
DX          Gypsies
```

Example 9

DA
750   Periodicals. Societies.
753   Yearbooks.
755   Sources and documents. Collections.
        Official.
757   Description and travel, see DA 850-878.
        History.
        Biography (Collective).
           Individual classed with special
           period, reign, or place.
758   General works.
  .1 Public men.
  .2 Rulers, kings, etc.
        House of Stuart, see DA758.3.S8.
           Early Stuarts, see DA783.5-9.
           Later Stuarts, see DA784-814.
           English sovereigns, see DA385-
           452.
  .3 Houses, noble families, etc.
        Including biographical memoirs.
           e.g. .M3 Earls of Mar.
                .S8 House of Stuart.
           For genealogy, prefer CS468-
           469, 479.
  .4 Women.

Example 10

LOCATING BOOKS ON THE LIBRARY SHELVES

Although, as mentioned earlier, Gates discusses the L.C. system, she does not convey in enough detail how the library user goes about employing this system to locate books on the shelf. What the user needs to know is that there is a direct relationship between the alphabetical-numerical arrangement of the classification system and the order in which the books are arranged on the shelves. The first or beginning letter in an L.C. classification book number tells the student what part or section of the library building to go to in initiating a search for the book. If there is a single letter, then the student should look at the beginning of that letter's section on the shelves. If there is a second letter, the student must trace through the section alphabetically to find the books having the appropriate pair of letters. Then it is necessary to begin tracing through for the numbers which follow the letter or letters in the top line of the number. To clarify, let's look at some specific examples. Back in Example 1 we had the number:

```
PS3511         PS              PS
A86Z65  or    3511     or    3511
              .A86Z65         .A86
                              Z65
```

The letter P tells us that this book is to be found in the P or language and literature section of the library. The S indicates that we are to trace through the P section alphabetically until we locate the S subdivision, having the numbers beginning with PS. Once we locate the PS's, there may be several thousand of them, since this is the division of literature for American literature. The next step is to look for the 3511's within the PS's.

It is necessary to caution students at this point that the 3511 is a whole number. One of the most frequent mistakes new users of the L.C.

system make is misinterpreting this as a number built upon 3 or 35, stopping at PS35 or more likely PS351 to look for this book rather than on over in the 3511's. In other words, this number sequence is of whole numbers; therefore, someone stopping at 35 or 351 when he should be hundreds of numbers further on will miss seeing this book, which should be a shelf or two over from 35 or 351. What one must do is continue on to the 3000's and within them to the 3500's and finally to the 3511's.

Once the student has found the PS3511's, the second line in turn must be traced through alphabetically and numerically in order to distinguish this particular PS3511 from all the others, because there should be many, perhaps as many as several hundred American literature books, in any but the smallest library, which fall into this division of the field. Books are arranged within the 3511's alphabetically and numerically according to the second line. Since the second line in our example begins with an A, this should be one of the first PS3511's. The A's in this second line will be arranged in numerical order in a decimal sequence according to the numbers which follow the A. That means an A851, for instance, will precede the A86, because .85 will precede .86 regardless of whether or not a number follows either the 5 or the 6. This is easier to see when the decimals are actually written in—as in the second part of the example. Nevertheless, even when the decimals are not written in, the books are arranged on the shelf as if they were. In this case the student has to remember that the decimal is there, even though it does not appear in the number.

When the A86's have been located, look in turn for the Z65. If there had been only one A86, no further addition to the number would have been necessary. But, apparently, the catalogers anticipated more than one, so the additional and final element in the number was added. When the student does find the Z65, there should be only the one book having that part of the number, because the

34

last element of the number is the portion unique
to its book. The number must be traced through
to this last section in order to spot the book
on the shelf. New users frequently ask if they
need to copy every line of the number, and of
course they do in order to follow through to the
last element in the number.

COMPUTER PREPARED INDEXES AND ABSTRACTS

Although computers are now used in the
preparation of the printed periodical indexes
familiar to undergraduates, such as the H. W.
Wilson Company's Readers' Guide to Periodical
Literature, the format of these traditional indexes, or the way in which their materials are
arranged, developed as it was in an earlier era,
has not been altered to reflect computer use. In
the Wilson indexes, and the New York Times Index,
articles are grouped under the subject words
which the indexers decide best reflect their content; hence, to find the appropriate subject word
or phrase is to find the articles themselves.

However, the number of headings under
which articles are listed is limited. One or two
subject headings or subheadings will be arbitrarily chosen to the exclusion of other possible appropriate terms. Therefore, the number of potential access points available to the user for any
particular kind of material is limited. This necessitates the provision of "see" and "see also"
references to let the user know under which terms,
from among several possible ones, articles have
actually been listed. These references take the
student from the word he or she is using for the
subject to the word or words the indexers have
used for grouping the articles on the subject.

In contrast, those printed indexes whose
organization is more reflective of computer retrieval formats provide multiple access points to
articles under a number of very specific terms or
descriptors in a separate subject index section.
This subject index section, in turn, refers the
user by number to what is called the main entry
or abstract section where more complete information on each article is provided under numbered
entries. This format evolved from the older abstracting publications as they added computerized
subject indexes of various kinds in the early
1960's. These publications had consisted of ab-

37

stracts of articles arranged under the broad subject divisions for their respective fields, making subject indexing necessary for very specific topics. Some limited subject indexing had been provided, but the development of automated indexing techniques made possible a greater variety of subject indexes to accompany the abstracts.

Thus, in the computer-oriented, printed indexes, subject headings and complete article references are placed in separate sections of the index rather than together, as in the traditional ones. This allows for more flexibility in providing subject access, because there is no restriction on the number of times an article can be referenced in the subject index section under very specific terms, referring the user by number back to the one listing in the main entry section. The complete information on each article, then, needs to be given only once under the numbered entry in the main section.

This main entry section is the largest division in any issue of the index. In addition to offering the author, institution where the research was conducted, title, periodical name, volume number, page, and date; the main entry includes, in many of these indexes, a list of all the subject descriptors used for the article in the subject index section. Also within the main entry section, all of these printed computer indexes provide a brief summary or abstract of the contents of the article. Descriptors and abstracts together provide the user with a concept of the overall subject scope and content of the article before going to the shelf to read it and aid the user in deciding whether or not an article can be used before it is searched for and read.

These abstracted entries in the main entry section are grouped and numbered consecutively under very broad subject categories that constitute the major divisions of the field covered by the index. This arrangement facilitates browsing and

provides the user an overview of new publications for an entire area of study. However, most users require much more specific subject access than the main entry section allows, so the separate subject index section is prepared with its specific terms or descriptors.

Finally, these computer indexes include a separate author index which gives the names of all the authors who prepared or aided in the preparation of the articles covered. This author section also refers users by number to the main entry section. Use of a separate, comprehensive author index makes possible many more references to articles by author than traditional indexing, which lists articles by author only if the individual is considered by the indexers to be a well-known authority.

The amount of information given on each article in the subject index section varies from one computer-prepared, printed index to another. In all of them, the subject index section refers the user to the main entry section by supplying the number by which each article is arranged in the main entry section. Some subject index sections give enough information on the source of the article that the user can go directly from the subject index to the shelf to read the article without ever looking at the abstract of it in the main entry section. Others provide no more than a few descriptive words or phrases accompanied by the abstract number which refers the user to the main entry section where complete bibliographical information on the article and its abstract will appear.

All of the computer prepared indexes feature sample entries and explanatory notes which will aid the student with characteristics peculiar to each. However, these explanations will be of only marginal value unless the overall concepts underlying the structure of these indexes are understood. The explanations which follow go beyond what is offered in the indexes themselves. Further, the indexes discussed were chosen not just to aid the students from the fields which the indexes cover, but also to provide examples of the type of computer indexing formats being made available in a wide range of fields today. No doubt more of this sort of indexing will be provided for additional fields in the future.

Current Index to Journals in Education, ERIC, 1969-

To clarify what we have said so far about these computer oriented printed indexes, let's take a look at some typical examples. The first one we will examine is the ERIC Current Index to Journals in Education. Generally referred to as C.I.J.E., this index is divided into five separate sections: (1) Source Journal Index, which gives an alphabetical list of the journals indexed together with publications and subscription information; (2) Main Entry Section; (3) Subject Index; (4) Author Index; and (5) Journal Contents Index. Following these is the list entitled New Thesaurus Terms.

Example 11 offers a portion of the Subject Index section from an issue of C.I.J.E. Note that the Subject Index section does give extensive information on each article, complete enough for you to go directly from it to the shelf to locate specific ones. However, as noted earlier, this index, and others like it, provide additional material in the Main Entry Section about the contents of each article which will help you to determine whether or not you really want to take the time to search for the article and read it.

Note that subject descriptors are given in boldface type on the left margin of each column. There are three such columns per page. Article references are arranged under the descriptors in numerical order according to their EJ numbers. The EJ number of each article is placed under it

Elkind (David)

Conservation of Volume in College Students:
  Challenging Elkind, Journal of Genetic Psychology v131 n2, pp183-94, Dec 77

                                        EJ 174 069

Emotional Adjustment

A Survey of the Reinforcements and Activities
  Elderly Citizens Feel Are Important for Their
  General Happiness, Essence: Issues in the
  Study of Aging, Dying, and Death v2 n1,
  pp5-24, 77
                                        EJ 173 187

Philosophical Views of Death, Health Education
  v8 n6, pp2-3, Nov-Dec 77
                                        EJ 174 622

Death and Dying, Health Education v8 n6, pp4-7,
  Nov-Dec 77
                                        EJ 174 623

Emotional Development

Beyond Despair and Disengagement: A Transact-
  ional Model of Personality Development in Later
  Life, International Journal of Aging and Human
  Development v8 n3, pp261-6, 77
                                        EJ 173 236

Suburbs: They May be Ruining Our Children--With
  No Help from Schools, American School Board
  Journal v165 n3, pp40-1, Mar 78
                                        EJ 173 621

Example 11

41

on the right margin of the column.

EJ numbers originate in the Main Entry Section where they are used to place all the articles in numerical order. In the Subject Index this number is used to refer people to the Main Entry Section.

Let's examine a specific reference in the Subject Index as shown in Example 11. Under Emotional Development note the last article entitled "Suburbs: They May Be Ruining Our Children." Following the title is the name of the journal, volume and issue numbers, the page numbers, and the date. Immediately under this reference is the EJ number: EJ 173 621. To find this article in the Main Entry Section trace through it numerically until you locate EJ 173 621.

The main entry for the EJ number is shown in Example 12. In the Main Entry Section, the article reference together with a fairly lengthy abstract is arranged with the EJ number above it on the left margin of the column. There are also three columns per page in this section.

The EA number given opposite the EJ number above this article reference is an ERIC in-house number and can be ignored by most users of the index. Immediately below these numbers is the title of the article.

The title is followed by the author's name which was not given with the entry in the Subject Index Section, then follow the name of the journal, underlined here, but given in italics in the index; volume number; issue number; page numbers; and date of the article. Immediately under the date are given the descriptors that were considered most representative of the contents of the article. Those descriptors, bearing asterisks, are the ones actually used as access points to this article in the Subject Index. The other descriptors are closely related but were not

MAIN ENTRY SECTION

EJ 173 620   EA 509 537
You Think Politics and Religion Are Touchy Topics?
Just Mention Mandatory Homework. Thompson,
Margery, American School Board Journal, v165 n3,
pp37-9, Mar 78
    *Homework, *Board of Education Policy, *Parent
    School Relationship, Elementary Secondary Edu-
    cation. Parent Participation, *Montgomery
    County Schools MD
Controversy broke out when a Montgomery County,
Maryland, school board member attempted to make
homework compulsory. Successful board policies
on homework are briefly discussed. (IRT)
Reprint Available (See p. vii): UMI

EJ 173 621   EA 509 538

Suburbs: They May Be Ruining Our Children--with
No Help from Schools. Wynne, Edward A., American
School Board Journal, v165 n3, pp40-1, Mar 78
    *Suburban Youth, *Suburban Schools, *Suburban
    Environment, *Interpersonal Relationship, *Emo-
    tional Development, Suburban Problems, Elemen-
    tary Secondary Education, Students
The experience-poor environment of the suburbs
have not trained our children to cope with diver-
sity and interpersonal stress, nor provided them
with constructive stimulation. Suburban schools
should be especially sensitive to the unique problems that confront their students and should re-
design their programs to deal with this challenge.
(Author/IRT)
Reprint Available (See p. vii): UMI

Example 12, Part 1

43

EJ 173 622   EA 509 539
How Not to Let Your Board and Superintendent Be
Hoodwinked by 'Research' Anderson, Bryce W.,
American School Board Journal, v165 n3, pp42, 44,
Mar 78
    *Educational Research, *Research Utilization,
    *Boards of Education, Elementary Secondary
    Education, Administrative Personnel, Board
    Administrator Relationship
Board members might be well advised to regard
with some skepticism most claims of "research
proves" advanced by administrators and faculty
representatives in promoting this or that new
program or method. At the very least, some prob-
ing into alternatives is in order. (Author/IRT)
Reprint Available (See p. vii): UMI

Example 12, Part 2

44

actually used in the Subject Index. They are included here to give a more complete description of the scope of the article. The remainder of the entry consists of the annotation or summary of the article plus information on the preparer of the summary and the availability of copies.

The Author Index, as you would expect, lists articles in alphabetical order under author's last names. With two co-authors, both names are alphabetized; but with more than two, only the first author's name is used for alphabetizing.

The Journal Contents Index is arranged alphabetically by the name of the journal and chronologically by the date of each issue. Instead of giving the page number on which the articles appeared in the original journal, the Journal Contents Index gives the EJ number of each and the articles are arranged in numerical order by EJ number.

New Thesaurus Terms consists of new subject terms or descriptors added to the ERIC system. This list updates their book The Thesaurus of ERIC Descriptors, a published list of all the subject descriptors used in the ERIC system. The Thesaurus is intended to aid researchers in identifying and selecting all the most appropriate terms for the subject material needed from the ERIC indexes.

Additional Computer Influenced, Printed Indexes

As techniques for preparing computer-assisted, printed indexing have evolved, subject index structures have become increasingly varied and intricate in order to reflect more closely the theoretical structures of the fields they cover. Subject indexing, then, is no longer limited simply to alphabetical arrangement alone. Abstract references can be grouped into categories meaningful to the specialists involved. The skeletal structure of such an index is shown in Example 13. The index is arranged in alphabetical order by major concepts with related sub-concepts alphabetized under them. Grouped under each sub-concept are the abstract numbers, shown as AN numbers in the example, for all the references which relate to that sub-concept.

```
MAJOR CONCEPT
   Related Sub-concept
         AN82412      AN92128      AN98981
         AN89875      AN93824      AN99209
   Related Sub-concept
         AN21838      AN62587      AN75829
         AN59282      AN65223      AN92873
MAJOR CONCEPT
```

Example 13

Example 14 illustrates still another means for structuring major terms and their related sub-terms.

Major Term	Related Terms	Abstract Number
TITANIC	ICEBERG	25892
	SUNKEN TRE	12958

Example 14

Even the structure of alphabetical subject indexing has been altered almost beyond recognition in some publications. Index users may encounter what is known as a KWIC or Key Word in Context Index, the format of which is especially disarming for new users accustomed to traditional indexing formats. The entries are in alphabetical order, but are alphabetized by

the words which run down the center of the column
rather than on the left margin of the column
where customarily placed. Sample phrases structured like those in a typical KWIC index are provided in Example 15.

Typical Structure for Key Word in Context Index

Related Words	Key Word	Related Words	Entry Number
AMES AUDOBON'S DRA	KING	FISHER HANGS I	21582
BERS OF CURT ACC	KING	ON THE FOX HU	98721
GAS ELVIS THE	KING	MADE SEVERAL	45289

Example 15

        The index is constructed from descrip-
tive phrases, one for each article, taken from
the major words in the author's title plus any
additional words the indexers deem necessary to
reflect the overall subject content of the article. Each principal word in the phrase is
centered and the phrase alphabetized by it. Each
centered word thereby becomes a key word and
access to the article is provided through alphabetizing it. Words which surrounded the key
word in the original phrase are divided into two
sets of phrases and placed on either side of the
key word to form one column of the index page.
Sometimes in this process of rearranging the
words, only fragments of words are left on either side of the centered or key word. These
phrases consisting of fragments of words and
whole words are provided to aid the user in
choosing the most appropriate references. There
are often several such columns per page in this
type of index. Structured phrases in the sample
Key Word Index in Example 15 were taken from the
following sentences: (1) Several members of
court accompanied the king on the fox hunt; (2)
Elvis the King made many appearances in Las
Vegas; (3) John James Audobon's drawing of the

47

king-fisher hangs in the South Gallery.

Providing such a rich variety of printed indexing structures greatly enhances the student's potential for locating all appropriate materials needed for a research project--once use of these indexes has been mastered. Whenever more than one type of subject indexing is provided within the covers of a printed indexing and abstracting publication, a thorough search for a topic in the publication usually requires looking for the topic in more than one of the variously arranged subject indexes. The student should, therefore, make every effort to investigate and use all of the subject indexes. Introductory pages will precede each type of index to explain its purpose and the techniques to be employed in its successful use. Self-teaching guidebooks and user orientation programs are also often made available with great success by the index publishers. In addition there should be library information staff members familiar with these subject index structures and available for orienting students to their use.

Chemical Abstracts, American Chemical Society, 1907-

Chemical Abstracts features a Keyword Index for its subject index. Example 16 shows sample entries from the Chemical Abstracts' Keyword Index. Note that the key words are given in alphabetical order on the left margin of the column. Related phrases are placed under the key words in alphabetical order, abstract numbers following each phrase. There are four columns per page.

Isocyanide
   lithium mol motion   31121g
   odor aerosol   30579a
   polypenylethyl model compd   24859a
Isocyanoacetylene
   rotation   33918w
Isocyanurate
   chloro dishwasher detergent   26431d
   polyurethane viodfree molding   P 25301z
   urethane copolymer molding   P 25360t
   urethane polymer manuf   P 25350q
Isoelec
   focusing bacitracin antibiotic sepn   30838j

Example 16

BIBLIOGRAPHIES

Guides to Reference and Subject Bibliographies

In order to locate the more specific references used in fields as specialized as those covered in graduate study, students need to learn what indexing and abstracting services like the ones just reviewed are provided in their own fields. Guides to reference books provide students an effective introduction to these advanced indexing and abstracting services by assembling lists of more materials than usually are pulled together under subject headings in the card catalog and many more than are listed in general works such as Downs and Keller's. In addition, these guides provide a description of the use and contents of each work, so that the student can learn at a glance which works should best suit his needs for a particular project. One of the most comprehensive of these guides is available in every library:

Eugene P. Sheehy. Guide to Reference Books. 9th ed. American Library Association, 1976.

This guide has served for decades in nine editions as the standard list of references. The coverage is so thorough that no two or three examples from the Guide can possibly be adequate. The student is advised to find through the index and table of contents the section, or sections covering his field and note the entries provided. Many libraries will have the works they own marked for the student's convenience. Library of Congress classification numbers were supplied for most books, further aiding in their location in the student's library. A convenient paperback edition will be available in 1980. Students will be able to keep their own copies at their fingertips.

There are several other volumes which

supplement and update the Guide.

A. J. Walford. Guide to Reference Material,
3rd. ed., 1973-1977; Vol. 1, Science
and Technology; Vol. 2, Social and His-
torical Science, Philosophy and Religion; Vol. 3, Generalities, Languages,
the Arts and Literature.

Walford's guide covers some works not
included in Sheehy's. In conjunction with
Sheehy's it can contribute toward a more complete picture of the references available in a
field. Walford's guide is rendered somewhat
less useful in the United States due to its
British origin.

American Reference Books Annual, 1970- Libraries Unlimited, 1970-
American Reference Books Annual, 1970-1976; a
cumulative index to subjects, authors,
and title. Libraries Unlimited. 1974.

This work, usually called ARBA, is organized by subject areas, having an evaluative
description of each work. ARBA includes significant reference works published in the last
year for each field; therefore, it effectively
supplements and updates Winchell and Walford.

Beyond these general guides to reference works, every discipline has its own specialized bibliographies and guides to research.
Some of these can be found listed in the general guides but not all of them are, and new
ones are constantly in preparation. Check for
new research guides in the sections of campus
bookstores set aside for your area of study.
The card catalog can also supply some of these
under such entries as: "Public Administration -
Research - Handbooks, Manuals, etc.;" or
"English language - Study and teaching - Bibliography."

Books in Print, Bowker, Updated annually.   2
            vols.   Authors; 2 vols. Titles.

        Lists by author and title all the books
that are available for purchase in English on
the American market including both brand new
works and older ones that have remained on the
market due to sustained sales. Though comprehensive, it does not provide descriptions of
works, nor make any value judgements or quality
screening.

Subject Guide to Books in Print, Bowker, Updated
            annually, 2 vols.

        Groups the works from Books in Print by
subject, thereby providing comprehensive lists
of all the books available for purchase in every
major field of study. The Subject Guide is a
useful supplement to the library's subject catalog, especially for recently published works,
some of which the student may wish to purchase
if otherwise unavailable. Campus book stores
are happy to take orders from Books in Print
and Subject Guide references. Again no quality
screening.

Forthcoming Books, Bowker, Updated bimonthly.

        Provides author and title lists of books
too new to have been included in Books in Print
or to be published in the very near future. Of
inestimable value for fields in which it is ab-
solutely necessary to keep one's research up to
date.

Subject Guide to Forthcoming Books, Bowker, Up-
            dated bimonthly

        Provides subject access to listings in
Forthcoming Books. Together they can offer invaluable guidance for research projects that re-

quire locating the latest material available.

Paperbound Books in Print, Bowker, Issued Spring
        and Fall.

        Provides author, title, and subject index-
ing for paperback books available for purchase.
With graduate students' budgets being as limited
as they inevitably are, knowing about the availability of paperback editions can be a life saver.
Most graduate students eventually accumulate their
own paperback library during their years of study.

Scientific and Technical Books and Serials in
        Print, Bowker, 1978.

        Pulls together appropriate references from
Books in Print, Subject Guide to Books in Print,
Ulrich's International Periodical Directory, Irregular Serials and Annuals, and Ulrich's Quarterly. Arranges all books by author, title, and subject. Can save graduate students in these fields
a great deal of time.

GUIDES TO THE LITERATURE

In addition to reference books, graduate students must also become familiar with the significant works that have contributed to the development of their respective fields. One of the principal goals of graduate education is that the student become firmly grounded in the literature of his field.

A number of attempts have been made to prepare lists of books that are considered to be the landmark works in major areas of study. Specialists from each field get together and select the titles to be included. Unfortunately, it is impossible to prepare such a list that would be universally accepted as complete and well balanced. Some specialists always claim that certain titles should have been omitted and others should have been added. But for the beginner such lists can offer a helpful overview of many esteemed works in his area of study. Later, as the student grows more familiar with the literature, he will become aware of gaps in the lists with which he started. These lists appear in two forms. Some, like the Harvard Lists, are limited to one area of specialization. Others are comprehensive in their attempt to provide the most significant works for every major area of study.

Books for College Libraries. American Library Association, 1st. ed. 1967; 2nd. ed., 1975.

Books for College Libraries is a comprehensive list. It includes over 40,000 titles prepared by subject specialists, academicians, academic librarians, and other advisors. Their aim was to prepare a core collection of the books essential for making any four-year college library adequate "to support an average college instructional program of good quality." Graduate students should already be familiar with some of the works provided for their area of

55

study, since the lists were intended for under-graduate library collections. However, just as graduate students have often failed to acquire library-use skills in their undergrauduate days, so have they frequently not been adequately exposed to the literature of their fields.

Both editions will be needed because significant older works omitted in the second edition can be found in the first, and important works too new for the first are listed only in the second. If a title is needed, but not available in the student's library, it can be ordered on interlibrary loan from another college library owning the book. The student may inquire about interlibrary loans at the information desk or reference desk in his library.

Choice. American Library Association, 1964-

The list in Books for College Libraries can be kept up to date and supplemented by Choice, a journal reviewing books for academic libraries. Organized by subject and including every field of academic endeavor, Choice reviews each month new and significant books recommended for purchase and, therefore, recommended for study by their student patrons and faculty. The reviews are prepared by subject specialists from all over the United States, so that each book is evaluated by an individual already familiar with the literature and with the intellectual context in which the new work has appeared. These reviews can alert the graduate student to interesting new ideas and trends of thought in his area of study. Choice is also a valuable source for locating new reference books with a separate section for new references in addition to the various subject sections.

Besides providing the valuable monthly reviews, Choice has published the Opening Day Collection which first appeared in 1965 with a revision in 1969-70. A third edition appeared beginning with the December, 1973, issue. The purpose of the Opening Day Collection was to determine as closely as possible what books every college and university library must have on its shelves in order to function adequately in its support of academic programs.

In addition to regularly updating the Opening Day Collection, Choice publishes in each May issue a list of the best academic books reviewed for a previous year. This list, entitled "Outstanding Academic Books" effectively updates and supplements the frequent revisions of these two compilations by providing each year an additional list of some of the best contributions that have been made in each field.

Two final services provided by Choice: a section which reviews new journals for academic libraries; and a monthly, special-feature, indepth bibliographic essay which discusses a topic of current interest accompanied by an extensive, highly selective list of recommended sources. Both of these latter services can prove invaluable to the student researcher.

Dissertation Abstracts International (originally Dissertation Abstracts), in two sections, A: Humanities and Social Sciences, B: Physical Sciences and Technology. University Microfilms, 1938- Plus C: European Dissertations, 1977-

This tool further brings graduate students up to date on research being conducted in their fields by listing and describing the contents of doctoral dissertations in these fields, since doctoral dissertations can be important sources of current information. Copies of dissertations on paper or on microfilm are available for purchase from University Microfilms. The abstracts have a computer-oriented, key word subject index and author index.

Related works which will supplement and aid in the use of Dissertation Abstracts International:

Comprehensive Dissertations Index, 1861-1972. University Microfilms, 1973. 37 vols.

Includes all dissertations in Dissertation Abstracts plus others. Computer-oriented key word and author indexes. Undertook a complete listing of all dissertations produced at American Universities for the years included plus some foreign ones.

Masters Abstracts: Abstracts of selected masters theses on microfilm. University Microfilms, 1962-

Cumulative Subject Index and Author Index to Volumes I-XV of Masters Abstracts. University Microfilms, 1977.

Subject and author computer index.

SPECIALIZED PERIODICALS AND INDEXES

In addition to listing important reference materials, the guides to research for specific disciplines usually include a list of the
specialized professional and research journals
for the field each covers along with the periodical indexes to be used in locating articles in
these journals. However, if the journals are not
listed, or if the list seems too abbreviated,
there is an additional directory which will be
helpful.

Ulrich's International Periodicals Directory,
        Bowker, 1932-

Updated biennially, with a quarterly
supplement between editions entitled Ulrich's
Quarterly, this directory is a near comprehensive world list of periodicals grouped under
broad subject areas with an index to more narrow
topics. Under the name of each journal the periodical index or indexes which cover it, are
given. Ulrich's can be checked against the periodicals ownership list in the student's library
and the necessary indexes located.

Supplemented and kept up to date by:

Irregular Serials and Annuals: an international
        directory. Bowker, 1967-

Biennial, beginning in 1972, alternately
with Ulrich's. Covers periodical type publications that appear annually, or less often, or
irregularly.

NONBOOK MATERIALS

Academic libraries are now acquiring significant research collections on microfilm and microfiche cards. Some of thse collections feature indexing or catalogs which are not integrated with the library's main card catalog, so the student must let an information librarian know his needs, in case some material is available from these collections. In addition, such software as films and filmstrips, phonograph recordings, cassettes, tapes, videotapes; and hardware like teaching machines, television, and other educational media are gaining significance for the researcher.

In the last decade college and university libraries have made available automated or computer indexing services which supply students and faculty with on-demand, computer produced lists of references on very specific research topics. These automated bibliographic services are offered as either an alternative to or a supplement for manual searching through printed indexes.

The computer produced printed indexes discussed earlier are the published counterparts of those automated indexing services which feature both printed and automated indexing of their data bases, thereby making manual searching through their printed index volumes possible as well as automated searching. The Current Index to Journals in Education (C.I.J.E.) is a typical example.

Automated retrieval services have been very enthusiastically promoted and not without good cause. Nevertheless, the beginning researcher must be cautioned about the strengths and weaknesses of these services in contrast with the strong points and weak points of manual searching through printed indexes. Basically, students should resist the temptation to use one type of indexing while ignoring the other. Students especially must be wary of those specialists who urge the use of one type to the exclusion of the other.

At some point in conducting a research project, the dilemma is inevitable: the student finds it necessary to decide whether to use printed indexes exclusively or whether to have an automated search run; or if the student has initiated the project with a computer search, the decision must be made as to whether or not supplemental work should be done in printed indexes. Much will depend upon the scope of the project. Exhaustive research projects require both manual and automated searching, and all but the smallest projects will benefit from both.

Although many automated services prepare printed indexes, not all of them do, making computer searching necessary for access to the resource references stored in them. However, prior to conducting an automated search, finding the bibliographic information on at least one or two appropriate sources can be invaluable in setting up a computer search. In the absence of a printed equivalent for a data base such sources could be found in other published indexes for the field and in related books before attempting specifications for the computer search.

Furthermore, initiating an automated search requires selection of the most appropriate subject terms or descriptors for the kind of information or topic the student seeks. The importance of choosing the proper descriptors in automated searching cannot be too strongly emphasized. Without the proper descriptors or combination of descriptors, the exact kind and number of references needed by the student cannot be retrieved.

Adequate placement of an automated search request, therefore, usually involves a discussion of the potential descriptors with the library in-

formation specialist or searcher who will process
the request through the data base. If the student
has already located examples of appropriate references as advised above, these can be invaluable to
the searcher in choosing the descriptors and de-
termining the most effective search strategy. The
searcher will make these final decisions in order
to retrieve the most closely related references
and, simultaneously, to prevent getting too many
irrelevant citations from the data base. Further
limitations that can be placed on a search include
whether or not to accept references in languages
other than English and how many years back the
references should go.

In deciding between printed and automated indexing the student must bear in mind that
with printed indexes the trial and error method
can be employed in the selection of subject terms.
One can readily and rapidly see the kinds of citations that are used under various indexing terms.
Further, once the proper citations have been located in the printed index, the student can go
directly to those sources in the library without
waiting time. Finally, some printed indexes provide information not available from any automated
ones.

However, as indicated in the earlier
section on printed indexes, the development of
search strategies by the user is necessary for
their successful use. The traditionally for-
mated indexes, for instance, tend to list article
references under only one heading and do not always give enough "see references" to anticipate
all the synonyms under which users will look.
Complicated structuring of the computer produced
subject indexes makes them particularly challenging in learning to use them. On the other hand,
with automated retrieval, responsibility for
search strategy shifts from the student to the
library information specialist conducting the
search. The student is, therefore, dependent upon
the searcher's skill for effective retrieval.

Great variation exists in effectiveness of retrieval from searcher to searcher on any one
project - so much so that there are now international competitions among searchers.

Although with automated indexes the computer, via the library information specialist,
does the searching for the student, there is always some waiting time for processing the request.
Also, students must pay for automated searches.
The price can range from $7.00 to $10.00 minimum
to $40.00 or more, depending upon the size of the
search; the number of years covered; the number
of data bases included; the number of citations
retrieved; whether or not abstracts are provided;
whether or not the search is on line; and whether
or not a print-out is made.

Once the student has received the references from an automated search, evaluation of them
is still necessary to determine whether they are
really appropriate for the project at hand. Only
the user can make the final value judgements in
terms of the unique needs of the project.

The student must bear in mind that in
manual searching of printed indexes some references are often found that are not retrieved in
automated searching, while automated searching
frequently produces some references not uncovered
by manual searching, even when the same data base
is involved. One must also remember that some
materials and publications indexed by one type
are not included in the other making it necessary
to use both whenever a thorough search is required.
When used together, then automated and manual
searching can reinforce and enhance each other.

THE GRADUATE ADVENTURE

Most people who have undertaken graduate study agree that while the requirements are much more demanding than on earlier levels, so also are the rewards proportionately greater. After experiencing the excitement of ever unfolding frontiers of knowledge - and in spite of the inevitable frustrations, these specialists have continued a lifetime of intellectual, emotional, and creative development that otherwise would have been virtually barred from them had they not undertaken graduate study. The highest purpose, then, of this Guide is to enhance the rewards of graduate research by providing a facility in using the tools of that research. Bon voyage!

.